More Fun Less Stuff

STARTER KIT

BETSY TAYLOR

CENTER FOR A NEW AMERICAN DREAM

Center for a New American Dream
6930 Carroll Avenue, Suite 900
Takoma Park, MD 20912
877-68-DREAM
newdream@newdream.org
www.newdream.org

Design by Gallagher/Wood Design
Illustrations by Tony Fitch

ISBN 0-9707727-0-X

This book is printed on 100% post-consumer recycled,
process chlorine-free paper using vegetable-based inks.

Acknowledgements

Many people contributed to this book. Thanks to all those at the Center for a New American Dream who took a turn at shaping and editing the numerous drafts of this publication. Special thanks to Communications Director and guru Eric Brown who served as the book's midwife (midhusband?). Thanks to lead co-writers Dave Tilford and Seán Sheehan. Pete Byer, Sara Pipher, Kim Posich and Jane Zeender each contributed ideas and time to this effort. Erin Yost provided invaluable support assistance. Thanks also to Patrice Gallagher and Amanda Wood, for their terrific design work; and Tony Fitch, for his wonderful illustrations.

The *More Fun, Less Stuff Starter Kit* was inspired in part by our board of directors — a group of authors, activists, and visionaries who always sing and share stories when they gather for business meetings. Our board Chair, Bob Engelman, reflects the values espoused in this book. He is a leading expert on population issues, drives a Toyota Prius hybrid automobile, lives modestly, and spends his free time playing Irish fiddle and hunting for waterfalls in the Washington metropolitan area.

I want to thank the many pioneers who continue to inspire and guide our work: Bill McKibben, Alan Durning, Donella Meadows, Amory Lovins, Paul Hawken, Jonathan Rowe, William McDonough, Norman Myers, Jerry Schubel, David Suzuki, Wendell Berry, Gretchen Daily, Herman Daly, Peter Raven, Winona LaDuke, and the many unsung heroes working to make a new American dream come true.

We are hugely indebted to the following foundations that provided general support funding to the Center for a New American Dream: Charles Stewart Mott Foundation, The

Educational Foundation of America, Merck Family Fund, The Nathan Cummings Foundation, The David and Lucile Packard Foundation, The Summit Foundation, Surdna Foundation, Town Creek Foundation, True North Foundation, Wallace Global Fund, and the Weeden Foundation.

Finally, thanks to you, our readers. We welcome your suggestions for improving this Starter Kit. Send us your comments at newdream@newdream.org or write us with your reactions. Give us your ideas on how to have more fun with less stuff!

Betsy Taylor

TABLE OF CONTENTS

Dear Friend,

BETSY TAYLOR

In this fast-paced world it's easy to wonder if our individual actions make any difference. If we embrace non-commercial values, live differently and consume responsibly, will it lead to a brighter future, even as others continue with business as usual? We at the Center for a New American Dream are convinced that the answer to this question is a resounding yes.

What You Do Matters

The fact is that the way you live creates ripple effects — in your family, your community, and workplace. In short, what you do matters. Each one of us has the capacity to bring about significant change in our individual quality of life and in the long-term future of the planet. And the good news is that many people are questioning the "more is better" definition of the American dream.

You Are Not Alone

We recently asked participants in our popular Step by Step action network what it was that they found most valuable about the program. The overwhelming response: "Knowing there are other people out there who share my belief on consumption and the environment and seeing how our collective action makes a huge impact."

Judging by your interest in this Starter Kit, it's clear you are part of a rapidly growing group of people who want to live consciously. You're not alone. Our website receives millions of hits a year. Over six hundred organizations are collaborating with us. While it's easy to feel discouraged by global environmental problems and excessive commercialism in our culture, it's encouraging to know that millions of Americans want to be part of the solution to these troubling trends. The possibility of a positive future is a reality.

The More Fun, Less Stuff Starter Kit

Now that you know that what you do matters and that you're not alone, what do you actually do? That's where this Starter Kit comes in. We've suggested "Nine Actions" for consuming wisely, practical tips for having fun without having to buy anything, and lots of resources to help you continue on your path. Let us know what's helpful and what's not. Let us know what we've left out and what you'd like to see more of. After all, you're not alone, and what you do (and think) matters.

With appreciation,

Betsy Taylor

Executive Director
Center for a New American Dream

MORE IS NOT ALWAYS BETTER

Before you immerse yourself in this Starter Kit, we encourage you to take a few moments to ponder some larger questions. People who ask the question, "how much is enough?" tend to be asking deep questions about the good life, about living in ways that reflect positive values, about how to do their part to ensure a healthy future for our children. In our rushed, noisy, fast-paced world, it is often difficult to just stop and reflect on our highest aspirations and dreams.

Getting Started

Indulge yourself in stopping. Slow down right now. Find a comfortable place to sit and, if you find it helpful, answer the following questions:

1 What do you most want in your life — right now and in the future?

_____

_____

_____

2 Why do so many people seem preoccupied with consuming more and bigger things? What's going on? What psychological, social, market, or other forces are driving excess consumption?

_____

_____

_____

3 What do you think about when you imagine the world fifty years from now? How will it be better? How will it be worse? What will the environment look like?

_____

_____

_____

_____

_____

_____

4 According to *Business Week* magazine, the average American is subjected to 3,000 commercial messages a day, through newspapers, television, radio, billboards, magazines, fashion logos, the Internet, phone solicitations, and more. In most cases, these ads suggest that we will find security, love, contentment, fun, meaning, respect, power and adventure by purchasing particular products. In short, the background noise of daily life in the new millennium boils down to this: buy your way to happiness. Make a list of those things in life that actually give you happiness and fulfillment. How many of them are material things? (It's OK if some are!)

_____

_____

_____

_____

_____

5 What more could you do to stay centered and focused on your deepest values and heartfelt aspirations? (Keep a journal? Meditate? Pray? Take time in nature? Slow down? Work less?)

_____

_____

_____

_____

_____

We hope this Starter Kit will help you be a wise consumer. We hope it will help you stay fully alive and in touch with your deepest wants and needs. We hope it will help you stay centered in a world that is out of balance.

PROTECTING THE ENVIRONMENT AND CONSERVING RESOURCES

"How much is enough?" has been a moral question for thousands of years. At the start of a new millennium, it carries new urgency. Though every product comes from the Earth and must return to it in one form or another, the environmental impacts are often unseen by the consumer and are much larger than we often imagine. One recent scientific study estimated that if every person in the world consumed like the average American, we'd need four more planets just to supply the resources and absorb the waste.

Consuming Like There's No Tomorrow

Consumption is not inherently bad — on the contrary, it's essential to human well-being. But the scale and patterns of consumption and production in the United States are contributing to major environmental problems. Finite resources like gas and oil are being consumed at an alarming rate. Renewable resources are being used much faster than they can be replenished. Forests are shrinking, fish stocks are declining, soil degradation is worsening and access to clean water is diminishing. We are also generating pollution and waste at a far greater rate than the Earth can absorb. Where does all this garbage go? Into the air and back into the Earth — or in some cases back onto the Earth. In fact, the highest geographic point on the eastern seaboard south of Maine is a pile of garbage — the Fresh Kills landfill on New York City's Staten Island.

> **If everyone develops a desire for the Western high-consumption lifestyle, the relentless growth in consumption, energy use, waste, and emissions may be disastrous.**
>
> —*National Academy of Sciences*

The Earth's Not in Balance and Neither are We!

The American work-and-spend culture has propelled us into an endless chase for more. In order to acquire "the good life," many Americans have increased the hours they work, intensifying stress levels and reducing the amount of time devoted to aspects of their lives they find truly rewarding.

- With less than five percent of the world's population, Americans consume 40 percent of the world's gasoline, 25 percent of the world's oil and 23 percent of the world's coal.

- Since 1940, Americans alone have used up as large a share of the Earth's mineral resources as all previous humans put together.

- The average American consumes nearly 750 pounds of paper each year, highest in the world.

- The average American generates over 1,600 pounds of trash per year — more than twice as much garbage as the average European.

It's easy to overlook the hidden costs of what economist Juliet Schor calls the "see, want, borrow, buy" way of life. But consider the following facts:

○ Per capita income has risen 62 percent since 1970, yet the percentage of Americans who report that they are "very happy" is no higher than it was in 1957.

○ The personal savings rate fell from 10.9 percent in 1982 to 2.4 percent in 1999. About two-thirds of American households fail to save anything in a typical year.

○ Credit card debt more than doubled during the 1990s. According to the Consumer Federation of America, nearly 60 percent of American households carried credit card balances in 1997, with the average balance exceeding $7,000. These households paid, on average, more than $1,000 each year in interest and fees.

○ By the mid-1990s, employed Americans spent over 140 hours more per year on the job than they did in the mid-1970s. Fully one-third of Americans say their lives are out of control.

○ In 1998, 1.4 million Americans declared personal bankruptcy — five times as many as in 1980 and more people than graduated from college that year!

Certain material goods can improve our quality of life, but our extraordinary preoccupation with acquiring more and bigger things can leave us out of balance. Consumer choices that are supposed to improve quality of life — bigger houses, bigger cars, the latest gadgets — often have hidden quality of life costs that we fail to account for: less free time, more debt, more stress. Our lifestyles also send a message to our children

that materialism is the ultimate definition of the good life. In a recent survey, 87 percent of parents said that children are already too materialistic and that excess commercialism is negatively influencing their kids' values. We need to recognize these hidden human costs of our consumer world.

In fact, many are beginning to realize that what they really want is not more stuff, but more free time and a deeper connection to their friends, family and community. There is a mistaken notion in this society that more material possessions result in greater happiness when, in fact, public opinion research demonstrates that meaningful work, positive relationships, public service, time in nature, and opportunities for leisure are sources of more lasting fulfillment.

How Much is Enough?

In an age of plenty there is a stunning division between the haves and the have-nots. While some literally have more than they know what to do with, many others struggle to pay bills, put food on the table, and hold down several part-time jobs to make ends meet. Overseas it's sometimes much worse, with millions of impoverished people subject to starvation, exposure and disease due to the vagaries of nature or politics. The difference between life in the U.S. and life in one of the poor countries is truly immense:

Runaway growth in consumption in the past fifty years is putting strains on the environment never before seen.

— United Nations Development Programme's Human Development Report 1998

✪ Globally, according to the United Nations, the 20 percent of the world's people in the highest-income nations account for 86 percent of private consumption expenditures; the bottom 20 percent a minuscule 1.3 percent.

✪ The average American consumes about 53 times more goods and services than someone from China. A child born in the U.S. will use 35 times more resources in his or her lifetime than a child born in India.

✪ The average American uses 106 times as much commercial energy as the average person in Bangladesh.

In this context, the questions "how much is enough?" and even "what is really important?" become profoundly challenging. Even if all six billion persons on Earth lived like the average American — which would cause catastrophic environmental impacts from mining, oil drilling, pollution and garbage disposal — we all would be still facing the same issues we Americans face today: what is really important? Do more goods lead to more happiness? Is a material culture worth a degraded environment? Or, instead, can we export a new American dream which emphasizes economic prosperity, material security, human well-being, a vibrant culture *and* a clean environment?

A Vision of a Positive Future

What's the New Dream?

While nobody can offer a perfect view of what a positive future will look like, the board and staff of the Center for a New American Dream do have a vision starting to take shape. We're all in this together, and if individuals, businesses, government and communities join hands, we can surprise the cynics, move the ambivalent, and feel authentic hope in our hearts. Here's what the new dream might look like:

❂ Responsible individuals, public agencies, businesses, universities, hospitals, restaurants, and non-profit groups will use their purchasing power to insist that products and consumer goods be designed and made in ways that are healthy for people and the environment.

❂ In response to this consumer pressure and demand, goods will be durable, made with recycled materials, designed for reuse and repair rather than obsolescence, and free of toxic substances.

✪ Governments will end subsidies for mining, ranching, advertising, factory farming, fossil fuel extraction, and logging. These subsidies slant the playing field away from sustainable alternatives and promote wasteful resource consumption. Removing subsidies for waste will prevent low-tech industries from undercutting industries that employ newer, cleaner technologies, and will provide consumers with more realistic choices.

✪ Fossil fuel will be replaced by renewable sources of energy and hydrogen cells, while atmospheric and solid waste will be dramatically reduced.

✪ Consumption will increase for the billions of poor people in Asia, Latin America, Africa, Central Europe and yes, here in the U.S., who need more material goods and security. International development banks, U.S. foreign aid programs, and other development agencies will give the most advanced and appropriate technology and environmentally friendly goods and agriculture to impoverished regions, avoiding many of the social and environmental problems associated with conventional development.

- Consumption of energy, meat, non-organic foods, and virgin wood products will decrease worldwide and policies will be enacted to give individuals and institutions incentives to consume wisely.

- The consumerist definition of the American dream will have some strong competition. More people will turn off commercial television, reject shopping as a pastime, and reclaim non-material pleasures. These people will attract others because their lives will exude fun, energy, and purpose. There will be a renaissance of dance, small plot farming, carpentry, music, visual arts, gardening, reading, hiking, bird-watching, and people will embrace moments of just "being" instead of always "doing." We will play more interactive games and get rid of our "Gameboys," and children will have enough time to ponder clouds, cloverleaves, and the sound of the wind.

- The values of instant gratification will be countered by values of deep empathy for fellow humans, caring for nature, and sharing.

Does this vision make sense to you? Does it seem realistic? Utopian? What would it take to build a society that looked this way? We welcome your feedback on how to build a new American dream that works for all of us. Drop us a card with suggestions or email us at newdream@newdream.org and let us know what you think.

Notes:

Suggestions for Being a Responsible Consumer

This section is designed to get you thinking about how you can make some simple but important changes in how you work, spend money, use resources, and spend time with friends and family. Use this section as a workbook. Jot down your ideas, and return to them from time to time to see how you've done.

"I like to shop. I won't deny it. But I've found new pleasure in shopping wisely. My local grocery store has started carrying locally grown vegetables and fruits. Sometimes they have organic food too. I like buying it. I've found websites and catalogs that help me buy recycled paper products, battery rechargers, low-flow showerheads, and organic cotton clothing. I feel a little smug when I buy something that I know is giving the planet some relief. And more and more, I'm trying to shop for things I really need rather than shopping when I feel depressed, lonely, or bored. I still enjoy shopping sometimes, but I try to be a smart shopper."

(Name withheld by request
San Francisco, California)

TIPS ON PURCHASES

Money is a tool. Each dollar we spend joins millions of others and helps determine the way products are made or harvested, how services are provided, and how workers are treated. Before you head to a store, take a moment to think about the way you spend your money. Are your purchases a response to wants, or needs? Are they based on importance, urgency, or impulse? Are they in harmony with your values, priorities, and goals?

Shopping for the planet and for human well-being takes time, and for many of us, time is scarce. So keep it simple. Don't start out by trying to be perfect, just take a step in the right direction. If thousands of consumers take small steps, industry will respond with better products and services.

✪ Seek out products that are locally produced. This supports your local economy and reduces energy consumption required by the global transport of goods. Farmers' markets are especially wonderful resources.

✪ Avoid products with excess packaging.

✪ If a product is electric-powered, look for an energy efficient model.

✪ Buy products made with recycled content, and try to bypass anything made from polyvinyl chloride, or "PVC" (labeled as "Number 3" plastic). Polyvinyl chloride is an environmentally damaging chemical.

✪ Whenever possible, look for labeling that lets you know the product is certified as environmentally friendly. These labels are moving into the marketplace — on wood products (FSC certification), seafood (MSC certification), coffee (labeled organic and shade grown), cotton, appliances, and other products. Labels can be helpful tools in selecting products that are environmentally preferable. (At the same time, don't blindly accept a product that calls itself "green" and doesn't offer any substantiation. It only takes a little practice to begin separating the green from the "greenwashing.") Look for the Green Seal and other labels offered by major environmental organizations.

How to Get Started Today

Each week or two, choose one product you buy regularly and explore its alternatives. If it's a food item, find an organic or locally grown version. If it's a household item, buy an environmentally friendly substitute — one that is energy efficient for example, or free of harmful chemicals. Buy in bulk to save money and packaging. If it's a paper product, find a 100% post-consumer recycled option. Don't give up if the more sustainable choices aren't immediately obvious.

For more information and to post your suggestions for others, go to www.newdream.org/money/.

ADDITIONAL RESOURCE: Co-op America's Green Pages, www.greenpages.org, (202) 872-5307. Learn more about companies and their products at www.responsibleshopper.org.

MY GOAL

IN THE NEXT MONTH, I WILL

_____

_____

_____

_____

THIS WILL BENEFIT MY QUALITY OF LIFE BY

_____

_____

_____

_____

THIS WILL HELP THE ENVIRONMENT BY

_____

_____

_____

_____

_____

"I recently moved to an 80 percent time university teaching contract so I could have more free time to do what I want. My colleagues were both surprised and somewhat interested in doing the same. I was recently sought out by a large organization for a possible new position. But why, I thought, should I give up my Colorado lifestyle for more money and a new title when it would cost me time from family, having to commute too much, and being pressured to live life like the wealthy are expected to live?"

Rich Feller
Colorado

TIPS ON WORK

North Americans are working more than ever, as new technologies bring about higher demand and expectations for more output, performance and service. For many of us, life has become a mad rush of meals on the run, commuter traffic and crushing workloads. Basic needs such as nutrition and sleep are feeling the squeeze, while stress-related health problems are mounting.

It's time to re-examine our cultural notions about work and success. Think about the number of hours each week you spend at work, commuting, and even decompressing at the end of a long day. How does that total look when compared to the number of hours you spend relaxing, socializing, reading, volunteering and caring for children?

Consider some alternatives to the typical work week: Flex-time lets you rearrange your work schedule to accommodate childcare or other activities. Part-time work may also be a viable option in a two-income household. The reduction in income is often offset by savings on daycare, transportation (including the cost of having an extra car), business wardrobes and take-out food. Job swapping with co-workers is an excellent way to learn new skills, and job sharing allows you to split responsibilities with a colleague and cut your office time in half. Finally, it may be possible to telecommute — work in your slippers from the comfort of your home while cutting down on the expense, hassle and pollution of the daily commute.

How to Get Started Today

Keep a "time diary" for just one week, recording the time you spend on activities such as shopping, driving, working, playing with kids, cooking, housework and family activities. When you're finished, sit down alone or with the important people in your life and figure out whether your current time allocation is in line with your values and priorities. If it's not, seriously explore possibilities for change. If you join a local study group with help from the Center, others might help you brainstorm on how to reconfigure your work life.

For more information and to post your suggestions for others, go to www.newdream.org/work/.

ADDITIONAL RESOURCES: New Road Map Foundation, PO Box 15981, Seattle WA, 98115, (206) 527-0437, www.newroadmap.org. Northwest Earth Institute, 506 SW 6th Avenue, Suite 1100, Portland, OR 97204, (503)227-2807, www.nwei.org.

MY GOAL

IN THE NEXT MONTH, I WILL

_____

_____

_____

_____

_____

THIS WILL BENEFIT MY QUALITY OF LIFE BY

_____

_____

_____

_____

_____

_____

THIS WILL HELP THE ENVIRONMENT BY

_____

_____

_____

_____

_____

_____

_____

_____

"Seven years ago, while living in the Washington, DC area, our car quit. So we quit cars. We walked more, relied on mass transit to commute, and took cabs when we loaded up at the grocery store. We found that we could do almost everything we needed to do without the enormous expense and bother of a privately owned automobile. We found we were calmer, became better planners, and learned a lot more about our neighborhood walking every day than we ever would have learned driving through it. The mental benefits of being able to ignore every car ad and store flyer outside our walking distance were enormous. We've since moved to another area. Our main priority: living somewhere we can continue living without a car."

Chris and Karalyn Middings
Vermont

TIPS ON TRANSPORTATION

Operating an automobile has enormous impacts on both the environment and quality of life. Not only does commuting by car devour fossil fuels at an alarming rate, but vehicle emissions are a major source of greenhouse warming and a variety of air pollution problems. With 5 percent of the world's population, the United States consumes 40 percent of the world's gasoline, and each gallon of gas burned pumps 19 pounds of carbon dioxide into the atmosphere. Currently, carbon dioxide emissions in the United States exceed 6 billion tons a year — over 20 tons per person. Taking steps to reduce your dependence on your automobile will provide great benefits for the Earth and for your own personal and family life.

It's time we start rethinking the purchasing and maintenance of our cars. When buying a car, look at models with high fuel efficiency, including electric or hybrid models. If you're not in the market for a new car, fear not. There are ways to care for your old car that protect the environment. For starters, keep your car well tuned, your tires properly inflated and your speed down. Recycle your oil and car parts. Consider buying retread tires. Americans dispose of nearly 300 million tires a year. Buying retreads keeps tires out of landfills.

How to Get Started Today

Drive less! Limiting your "windshield time" is a simple way to reduce the amount of environmental damage inflicted by cars. Carpool, telecommute, bike, or use public transportation at least once a week if possible. Combine errands for fewer trips. Once you reduce your reliance on cars, you'll realize how many other transportation options exist. If driving less just isn't an option in your area, buy a fuel-efficient car and press your elected officials to offer better transportation options, or try to change your work or living situation to avoid long drive times.

For more information and to post your suggestions for others, go to www.newdream.org/transport/.

ADDITIONAL RESOURCES: American Council for an Energy-Efficient Economy's Green Book: www.greenercars.org and the Green Car Campaign: www.greencar.org.

MY GOAL

IN THE NEXT MONTH, I WILL

_____

_____

_____

_____

THIS WILL BENEFIT MY QUALITY OF LIFE BY

_____

_____

_____

_____

_____

THIS WILL HELP THE ENVIRONMENT BY

_____

_____

_____

_____

_____

_____

_____

_____

_____

_____

_____

"In the past few years I've changed my diet and other aspects of my lifestyle to make my world and the planet a healthier place. First of all, I've joined a community-supported farm collective and I also go to a Farmers' Market from May through November to get my produce. During the winter months, when local produce is not available as much, I use more cabbage and winter squashes in my diet. I try to buy organic produce and other organic food products whenever possible. I choose locally grown and produced foods in most cases, especially when I know the grower or producer."

Barbara Fingold
Address Withheld

Tips on Food

Food is our most fundamental connection to the Earth. Selecting what you eat requires knowledge and care, particularly when you factor in the environmental impacts of agrculture and food distribution. But there are a number of ways to eat well while protecting the planet.

First, try eating lower on the food chain. That is, instead of eating the meat of animals which were fed large quantities of grain or other foods, eat these foods directly in the forms of potatoes, rice, wheat, etc. Beef production represents a highly inefficient use of resources. Hundreds of gallons of water go into producing a single burger, and each pound of beef requires several pounds of grain. Beef production can also have huge environmental impacts. The waste produced by factory feedlots (not only for cattle, but for pigs and chickens) is enormous. In the United States, cattle damage sensitive riparian areas while in Central and South America millions of acres of tropical forest have been cleared for grazing.

Whenever possible, eat a local diet by growing your own food or by supporting local farmers, food stores, and co-ops. You will eat higher quality foods, strengthen your community, and reduce transportation and energy costs due to shipping food.

If you do eat meat, try to find organic, hormone-free open range meat products. When eating fish, follow the guide from the Monterey Bay Aquarium on seafood (www.mbayaq.org). Try to regain the pleasure of making your own bread using organic grains and flours.

Finally, pay attention to how food is packaged. Packaging waste makes up fully one-third of our municipal waste stream by weight. Even if you're eating organic food, it is not as Earth-friendly if it comes wrapped in layers of unnecessary plastic and cardboard.

How to Get Started Today

Pack "garbageless" lunches consisting of fresh food in reusable containers accompanied by cloth napkins. Try one extra meatless meal and at least one organic fruit per week. Fruits carry heavy loads of pesticides and consumer demand for organic fruits will create incentives for more sustainable agricultural production.

For more information and to post your suggestions for others, go to www.newdream.org/food/.

ADDITIONAL RESOURCE: The Food Alliance, 1829 NE Alberta, Suite 3, Portland, OR 97211, (503) 493-1066, www.thefoodalliance.org.

MY GOAL

IN THE NEXT MONTH, I WILL

_____

_____

_____

_____

THIS WILL BENEFIT MY QUALITY OF LIFE BY

_____

_____

_____

_____

_____

_____

THIS WILL HELP THE ENVIRONMENT BY

_____

_____

_____

_____

_____

_____

_____

_____

_____

_____

_____

_____

"We installed compact florescent bulbs and timers for all lights that are on for long periods of time. We lowered our thermostat setting two degrees in the winter during the day and eight degrees at night to cut back on natural gas consumption. We made a solar night light for our back door from a lawn light kit. We participate in our local electric company's "Nature First Program," where they can cycle our power off as needed to reduce reliance on high polluting generation sources."

Mike and Linda Lenich
South Holland, Illinois

TIPS FOR USING LESS ENERGY

In this era of relative economic prosperity, houses are getting bigger and their overall efficiency is declining. We're engaged in "conspicuous energy consumption," notes Seth Dunn of the Worldwatch Institute. Furnaces and air conditioners represent the biggest energy drains, followed by water heaters. Overuse of lighting — which is responsible for a quarter of all American electricity consumption — is also a significant problem.

So what can we do? For starters, consider home size when buying a house. Don't pay for more space than you need; you'll thank yourself when lower heating and cooling

bills arrive. If you live in an older house, make sure your home is well insulated. Twelve times as much heat escapes through a single window pane as through a wall. Make sure the doors, windows, pipes and outlets in your home are weather-stripped, sealed and caulked. The cracks and gaps in the average American home contribute up to 15 percent of home heating energy. When purchasing new appliances, invest in energy-efficient models (look for the "Energy Star" label).

How to Get Started Today

Install energy-saving compact fluorescent light bulbs in at least three commonly used fixtures. These bulbs last 10 times longer than regular incandescent bulbs and use only one-fourth the energy.

For more information and to post your suggestions for others, go to www.newdream.org/home/.

ADDITIONAL RESOURCES: EPA Energy Star Program, www.epa.gov, c/o EPA, Washington, DC, 20460, (888) 782-7937 and the Rocky Mountain Institute, 1739 Snowmass Creek Road, Snowmass, CO 81654, (970) 927-3851, www.rmi.org. Also, check out the World Resources Institute's new website, www.safeclimate.net.

MY GOAL

IN THE NEXT MONTH, I WILL

_____

_____

_____

_____

THIS WILL BENEFIT MY QUALITY OF LIFE BY

_____

_____

_____

_____

_____

_____

THIS WILL HELP THE ENVIRONMENT BY

_____

_____

_____

_____

_____

_____

_____

_____

_____

_____

_____

_____

"We are eliminating our boring lawn. It's going wild at the moment, but we may try to be a little more ambitious in the future and replace it with native wildflowers. We have planted some trees and bushes that are native to our area (on the advice of a local organic/low-impact horticulturist); they use less water and are even considered a capital improvement to our property."

Carolyn Lengel
Garrison, New York

Tips for Using Less Water

While in many parts of the world the supply of fresh water is threatened by increasing demand, in America billions of gallons of water are wasted each year. (The average American uses 182 gallons of water each day; by contrast, the average resident of Senegal uses only 7 ½ gallons per day.) The world's fresh water supply is finite, and it's crucial that we reduce consumption to conserve this resource.

Inside the house, install low flow showerheads and low volume flush devices in your toilets. (Tip: if you fill a one-liter bottle of water and place it in your tank, you will use one less liter of water every time you flush.) Inexpensive devices are also available which allow you to turn off a shower or sink momentarily, then restart its flow without affecting temperature or pressure. Outdoors, if you have a yard, rethink your landscaping. About 35 percent of household water use is attributed to lawn care. Switching to a landscape dominated by bushes and shrubs, as opposed to grass, could reduce lawn watering by 80 percent. Plant indigenous trees and flowers, which require less water. If you must water your lawn,

do it at night; less water will evaporate during the cool
evening hours.

How to Get Started Today

You can cut your water consumption by as much as 75 percent if you turn off the tap while you're brushing your
teeth or shaving. Showering (unless you linger) also uses less
water than baths.

*For more information and to post your suggestions for others,
go to www.newdream.org/home/.*

ADDITIONAL RESOURCES: Several regionally-based websites
provide excellent water conservation tips. Check out the
Fairfax County (VA) Water Authority site: www.fcwa.org,
the Clark Country (WA) Public Utilities "Tips" site:
www.clarkpud.com/tips.htm, and the fact sheets on the Okla-
homa Department of Environmental Quality site:
www.deq.state.ok.us/.

MY GOAL

IN THE NEXT MONTH, I WILL

_____

_____

_____

_____

THIS WILL BENEFIT MY QUALITY OF LIFE BY

_____

_____

_____

_____

_____

_____

THIS WILL HELP THE ENVIRONMENT BY

_____

_____

_____

_____

_____

_____

_____

_____

_____

_____

_____

_____

"When I was working in a corporate accounting department, I was appalled at the amount of junk mail our 20 person office received. Since most of my officemates were unwilling to take the time to get themselves off mailing lists, I set myself up as the office point-person for junk mail. People dropped their unwanted mail off at my desk, and once a week or so I went through the pile and contacted the senders, asking that they remove our employees from their mailing lists.

Although I did this primarily to save trees, it worked to everyone's advantage: companies no longer wasted money mailing us information we would never use, and our employees ended up with less mail to sort through."

Deborah Underwood
San Francisco, California

TIPS FOR GREENER OFFICES

When shifting your consumption patterns at the office, think paper and energy. In 1996, office copiers in the United States churned out more than 800 billion sheets of paper, computer printers nearly as many. Contrary to earlier predictions, computers and email have actually *increased* the amount of paper used. Paper has three major environmental impacts: destruction of forests, dioxin production in the chlorine bleaching process that harms fish and causes cancer in humans, and disposal. (Landfills are nearly one-third paper waste.) Also, office machines are as guilty of energy overuse as household appliances.

Buy chlorine-free, high recycled content printing and writing paper and tissue products. If a sheet of paper is blank on one side, reuse it for in-house drafts and photocopies. Always try to print letters and reports on both sides. Reuse

envelopes, bags and mailers. Recycle office paper, aluminum, steel, glass, newspapers, and cardboard. Stock your office kitchen with glasses, plates, and silverware rather than using disposable items.

How to Get Started Today

Don't waste paper, and turn off lights and office machines when not needed, including turning off computers overnight. (Don't worry about harming the hard drive — according to the Rocky Mountain Institute, a computer would have to be turned off every five minutes to do damage!)

For more information and to post your suggestions for others, go to www.newdream.org/tech/.

ADDITIONAL RESOURCES: *ACEEE Guide to Energy Efficient Office Equipment*, 2140 Shattuck Avenue, Berkeley, CA, 94704, (510) 934-4212, www.aceee.org, and *The Smart Office* by A.K. Townsend, GILA Press, P.O. Box 623, Olney, MD 20830, (301) 774-0917. For sources of sustainably-produced paper, check out www.woodwise.org.

MY GOAL

IN THE NEXT MONTH, I WILL

_____

_____

_____

_____

THIS WILL BENEFIT MY QUALITY OF LIFE BY

_____

_____

_____

_____

_____

_____

THIS WILL HELP THE ENVIRONMENT BY

_____

_____

_____

_____

_____

_____

_____

_____

_____

_____

_____

"I like to give dramatic, unusual experiences, not stuff, for gifts. For example, I traditionally take my nephew camping or create a treasure hunt for his birthday. For the treasure hunt, I make up rhyming clues to challenge him and head him off in all directions. I started this when he first learned to read, with clues leading around his house to a small gift. Now, at 13, his clues take him all through our downtown and require him to interact with other people in funny scenarios. I overheard him telling a friend how cool a treasure hunt is. The friend said, "Wow, there must be a really big gift at the end." Then he said, "No, the present is the hunt!" The cost is zero or close to it, and it is a more creative and personal way to express love than by going out and buying stuff kids probably don't need anyway."

Carol Pimentel
California

TIPS ON GIFT GIVING

Gift giving has become increasingly commercialized and overemphasized. From birthday goodie bags to wedding gift registries, our holidays have become focused on "stuff." The average American family now spends close to $900 on Christmas gifts, then spends six months paying off holiday credit card debt. Our commercial culture tries to make us think that the value we place on a person is directly tied to the amount of money we spend on him or her. Fortunately, giving doesn't have to be this way. There are many options available to help you move away from the consumer gift giving frenzy.

Alternative, non-material gifts can offer wonderful, creative expressions of love and friendship. Consider giving

someone a gift of time, such as a candlelight dinner, massage, or day of hiking. Offer to share a gift of experience — teach a skill that you possess, such as cooking, carpentry, music or sports. Treat your friends and neighbors to homemade gifts, including framed photographs, family recipe books and favorite baked goods. Donations to charitable organizations in honor of friends and family are also meaningful gifts.

How to Get Started Today

Plan ahead for the next holiday season. Make an audio tape of an older member of your extended family. Have the person reminisce about childhood, about other family members, and about life at an earlier time. Make copies of the tape and share it with all family members as a holiday gift.

For more information and to post your suggestions for others, go to www.newdream.org/holiday/.

ADDITIONAL RESOURCE: Alternative Gifts International, (800) 842-2243, www.altgifts.org. *Hundred Dollar Holiday* by Bill McKibben, Simon & Schuster, Inc.

MY GOAL

IN THE NEXT MONTH, I WILL

_____

_____

_____

_____

THIS WILL BENEFIT MY QUALITY OF LIFE BY

_____

_____

_____

_____

_____

_____

THIS WILL HELP THE ENVIRONMENT BY

_____

_____

_____

_____

_____

_____

_____

_____

_____

_____

_____

"Recently, four friends, one dog and I piled into one truck (to save fuel), and drove three hours away to an amazing set of natural hotsprings in Idaho (our alternative energy heat source for the weekend). We utilized the Earth's natural geothermal energies to full effectiveness throughout the weekend. The boys, usually all meatatarians, lived on my vegetarian bean and rice burritos, ramen and bagels. For additional entertainment, we hiked around the surrounding hillsides and made fun of the dog's antics. Who needs TV! Last but not least, I made sure that upon our return, all the beer cans were recycled. None of us are rich — a mix of college kids and blue collar bums, but not one of us would trade a blue sky day in the hotsprings for another day of work."

Michelle Anderson
Missoula, Montana

TIPS ON FAMILY AND RECREATION

Now that you're shifting your consumption patterns and slowing the pace of your life, you've got extra time to spend with family and friends. Great. So, how can you plan trips and other recreation activities in a way that protects the Earth? For starters, take time to revel in the beauty and peace of the natural world. On weekends, take day-long bike trips instead of road trips. Organize friends and neighbors into pick-up softball or volleyball games. Invite several families for a walk along a hiking trail. Join clean-ups of local parks and waterways. On rainy days, instead of turning on a video, play board games, tell stories, or dust off a favorite cookie recipe.

For vacations, think about taking your next holiday locally. Minimize air travel, which uses 40 percent more fuel per passenger-mile than an automobile. Explore your home town or state instead. When you travel long distances, take trains or drive instead of flying.

How to Get Started Today

Pick a day in the next month to spend with friends or family in a park, forest or natural area. Pack a picnic. Take a short hike. Leave the portable video games and cell phones behind. Walk at a modest pace. Pick a new place to visit once a month with people you love being with. Make some memories.

For more information and to post your suggestions for others, go to www.newdream.org/home/.

ADDITIONAL RESOURCE: The Rails-to-Trails Conservancy has information about thousands of miles of hiking/biking trails nationwide. Call (202) 331-9696 or click on www.railtrails.org.

MY GOAL

IN THE NEXT MONTH, I WILL

_____

_____

_____

THIS WILL BENEFIT MY QUALITY OF LIFE BY

_____

_____

_____

_____

_____

THIS WILL HELP THE ENVIRONMENT BY

_____

_____

_____

_____

_____

_____

_____

_____

TURN THE TIDE:
NINE ACTIONS FOR THE PLANET

Wouldn't it be great if you could make very specific lifestyle changes and immediately know the impact of those changes? And better yet, if you knew that you weren't alone — that thousands of other people were taking the same actions — because you could see the result of everyone's collective work?

Well, now you can!

We know we can have a significant positive impact on the environment if we can encourage many people to take small steps together. Of course, they have to make changes that matter — that conserve resources and protect the environment. We have to take actions that are specific and achievable within the constraints of our busy schedules, yet we must also incorporate broader changes in other aspects of our lives. Finally, enough people must participate to collectively make a large impact. Needless to say, the more we know about the results of our actions, the more we'll be motivated to keep going.

With this in mind, the Center created "Turn the Tide: Nine Actions for the Planet." We asked leading scientists and environmental experts to recommend some steps that Americans could take that would have a significant positive environmental impact. Our goal was to select consumer actions that would save forests, protect endangered species and stem global warming, among many other environmental benefits.

We've compiled a list of powerful actions that most people can take without significant inconvenience. When these nine little actions are taken together by thousands of us, it will have a significant impact on our environment.

For example, if just 1,000 of us take these actions, over one year we will save a collective 48 million gallons of water, 170 trees, 12,250 pounds of sea life, and prevent the emission of four million pounds of climate-warming carbon dioxide!

Counting Change

We ask you to join us in taking these steps over the coming year. Log onto www.newdream.org, set up your own personal workspace, and watch as our online calculator tallies the environmental impact of your reported actions. We'll also keep a running total of the combined savings of all Turn the Tide participants.

Of course, it's okay if you don't have web access — grab a calculator (or a pencil and paper) and use the next few pages as your workbook. Just be sure to report your action to us, so we can count your impact in our collective tally. You can do this by sending your results to: Center for a New American Dream, ATTN: Turn the Tide, 6930 Carroll Avenue, Suite 900, Takoma Park, MD 20912. We'll calculate the impact of your action and keep you posted with periodic communications and through our quarterly newsletter, *Enough!*

Together, we can do more than dream. We can make a difference right here and now.

THE POWER OF INDIVIDUAL ACTION

It's important to remember that these nine actions are important steps consumers can take in building a new American dream, but we will also need businesses to 'close the loop' and manufacture goods as cleanly and efficiently as possible. We will need governments to embrace green choices in their own institutional decision-making and eliminate policies that promote wasteful consumption. But it is also important to recognize the potential of individuals, in taking these and successive steps, to prod businesses and governments into doing their part.

4 ACTIONS FOR YOU...

1. Skip a car trip each week.

Since 1960, the American population has increased by 50 percent but the miles we travel each year have more than tripled. And 90 percent of our trips are in an automobile or light truck. Americans consume 40 percent of the world's gasoline and emit more climate-changing gases than China, Japan, and India combined! Transportation, overwhelmingly in automobiles, is responsible for about a third of American greenhouse gas emissions. The car culture is also a main driver of sprawl and the ensuing habitat loss. We can do better. By reducing your drive time and miles on the road, you can have an immediate positive impact on the environment.

Choose one trip you make on a weekly basis. Then decide how to get that task done without your car — whether it be by biking, taking public transportation, carpooling, telecommuting, or simply eliminating an expendable trip. Skipping a weekly 20 mile trip represents less than a 10 percent decrease

in the average American's driving and can reduce your weekly carbon dioxide emissions by more than 18 pounds. If only 1,000 of us take this action, we will prevent nearly a million pounds of carbon dioxide from being released into the atmosphere each year! Together we will give the climate a break and improve air quality while preventing traffic congestion, sprawl, and habitat loss.

❏ The weekly trip(s) I am skipping totals _____ miles per week. My car gets _____ miles per gallon (if you are unsure, enter the American average of 21.5 mpg).

Enter the above numbers into your personal workspace at www.newdream.org or, for those of you keeping score at home, use the following formula and record your results on the chart on page 79.

_____ miles skipped per week x 1,021 ÷ _____ car's mpg = _____ pounds of carbon dioxide saved each year

❏ I have not taken this action yet.

❏ I don't own a car and don't take any regular car trips. Congratulations! Not driving saves nearly 12,000 pounds of carbon dioxide per year compared to the average American.

2. Eat one less beef meal each week.

Meat production is extremely resource-intensive — livestock currently consume 70 percent of America's grain production! According to the Union of Concerned Scientists, grazing

accounts for 800 million acres (40 percent) of U.S. land, and 18 percent of all water consumption is devoted to producing feed for livestock.

Feedlot beef is particularly wasteful. Producing one pound of feedlot beef in California, for example, requires five pounds of grain and over 2,400 gallons of water. It also results in the erosion of five pounds of topsoil. To make matters worse, poultry, hog, and beef factory farms also lead to agricultural waste runoff — a major source of water pollution.

If you want to go vegetarian or switch to organic, freerange meat, great! But you can have a measurable impact by simply replacing one steak, plate of spaghetti and meatballs, beef lasagna or a trip to the local fast food joint with a nice vegetarian meal once a week. If only 1,000 of us take this action, we will save over 70,000 pounds of grain, 70,000 pounds of topsoil and 40 million gallons of water each year!

> ○ Amount of grain we'll save if only 1,000 of us take this step:
> 70,000 pounds per year
> ○ Amount of grain eaten by 273 sub-Saharan Africans:
> 70,000 pounds per year

> In other words, if a family of four eats one grain-based vegetarian meal each week in place of a beef-based meal, they will save more grain than is eaten by the average person in sub-Saharan Africa in an entire year.

❏ I am replacing ____ meal(s) of beef with vegetarian
   meals each week.

Enter the above numbers into your personal workspace at www.newdream.org or, for
those of you keeping score at home, use the following formula and record your results
on the chart on page 79.

____ beef meals skipped x 40,600 =
         _____ gallons of water saved each year

____ beef meals skipped x 300 =
         _____ pounds of carbon dioxide saved each year

____ beef meals skipped x 70 =
         _____ pounds of grain saved each year

❏ I have not taken this action yet.

❏ I can't take the beef action because I'm already a
   vegetarian.

❏ I'm not a vegetarian but I can't take the beef action
   because I already eat virtually no beef.

   Congratulations! Eating vegetarian meals instead of
   beef saves over 150,000 gallons of water and about
   260 pounds of grain each year.

3. Don't eat shrimp.

Today, nearly 70 percent of the world's fisheries are fully fished or overfished, and about 60 billion pounds of fish and seabirds die each year as "bycatch" — animals caught accidentally as a result of wasteful fishing techniques. Consider shrimp consumption, which in the U.S. has doubled over the last decade to the tune of 1 billion pounds per year. For every pound of shrimp caught, over five pounds of marine life is killed, including endangered sea turtles. And shrimp farms are no better, spilling pesticides into surrounding waterways and destroying over a quarter of the world's mangrove forests. If only 1,000 of us stop eating shrimp, we can save over 12,000 pounds of sea life this year alone. If we all do this and follow the recommendations of the Monterey Bay Aquarium's Seafood Guide (see www.mbayaq.org), we will help restore oceans and fisheries for future generations.

❏ I am giving up shrimp. I am saving 12 pounds of sea life per year, including endangered sea turtles, and helping protect the world's mangrove forests.

Enter the above numbers into your personal workspace at www.newdream.org or into the chart on page 79.

❏ I haven't taken this action yet.

❏ I can't give up shrimp because I don't eat it to begin with.

Congratulations! Not eating shrimp saves 12 pounds of sea life per year, and protects endangered coastal habitats.

4. Declare your independence from junk mail.

The world's forests are feeling the strain of unsustainable demand for wood and paper. By weight, paper products also comprise nearly one-third of all waste going into American landfills. Bulk mail, a substantial chunk of our paper waste, is especially troubling because it is often unsolicited and thus leaves citizens to dispose of materials they did not choose to consume in the first place. Catalogs and other direct mailings account for 5.2 million tons of waste each year and are recycled at a paltry rate of 19 percent, leaving over 4 million tons to clog landfills. That's 340,000 garbage trucks filled to the brim with nothing but bulk mail!

It doesn't have to be that way. You can call or write catalog houses to cancel unwanted or duplicate catalogs or to be placed on a restricted annual mailing list. You can also write to the mail preference services listed on page 69. Be sure to do so not only for yourself but also for your home's past residents. If only 1,000 of us succeed in halving our personal bulk mail, we will save 170 trees, nearly 46 pounds of carbon dioxide, and 70,000 gallons of water each year.

❏ I am taking steps to halve my receipt of bulk mail. I am saving 1/6 of a tree, 46 pounds of carbon dioxide, and 70 gallons of water each year.

Enter the above number into your personal workspace at www.newdream.org or into the chart on page 79.

❏ I have not taken this action yet.

❏ I've already taken the recommended steps to reduce bulk mail.

Congratulations! Complete elimination of bulk mail saves 1/3 of a tree, 92 pounds of carbon dioxide, and 140 gallons of water each year.

DECLARE YOUR INDEPENDENCE FROM JUNK MAIL

Our website features a form that will generate letters for you to print out, sign, and mail to marketing preference organizations. You can find this form at www.newdream.org/junkmail/.

If you don't have easy access to the web, you can just write a short note to the following organizations:

Mail Preference Service
Direct Marketing Association
P. O. Box 9008
Farmingdale, NY 11735-9008

Polk "Opt-Out Program"
List Order Services
1621 Eighteenth Street
Denver, CO 80202

Make sure your letter or postcard contains the following:

1. a request to the effect of "Please take my name off all marketing lists. Here is the information you requested:"

2. your first, middle and last name, current mailing address, and your phone number

3. your signature

OTHER TIPS

- To eliminate all those unsolicited "pre-approved" credit card offers, call toll-free (800) 353-0809, select "remove name permanently," and leave required information.

- Call unwanted catalogs and ask to be taken off their mailing lists.

- Whenever you order a product or otherwise share your address, always remember to say, "Please do not sell, rent, or trade my name."

...AND 4 ACTIONS FOR YOUR HOUSEHOLD...

5. Replace four standard light bulbs with energy-efficient compact fluorescent lights (CFLs).

Electricity production is the largest source of greenhouse gas emissions in the U.S., and lighting accounts for about 25 percent of American electricity consumption. If only 1,000 of us each replace four standard bulbs with CFLs, we can prevent the emission of five million pounds of carbon dioxide and reduce our electricity bills by more than $100,000 over the lives of those bulbs.

❏ My household is replacing _____ standard bulbs with CFLs because of Turn the Tide.

Enter the above numbers into your personal workspace at www.newdream.org or, for those of you keeping score at home, use the following formula and record your results on the chart on page 79.

_____ CFLs x 262 =
     _____ pounds of carbon dioxide saved each year

❏ I haven't taken this action yet.

❏ I didn't take the CFL action because all the light fixtures in my household are already fitted with CFLs.

❏ My household already had _____ CFLs to begin with. Congratulations! Each CFL saves about 262 pounds of carbon dioxide per year.

6. Move the thermostat 3° F.

Heating and cooling represents the biggest chunk of our home energy consumption. Consider replacing your old furnace or air conditioner with a much more efficient new model. But if that isn't possible in the short term, do the obvious. Mellow out on the climate control! Just by turning the thermostat down three degrees in the winter and up three degrees in the summer, you can save an average of 7.7 million BTUs of energy and prevent the emission of nearly 1,100 pounds of carbon dioxide annually. If only 1,000 of us shift three degrees, we will prevent over a million pounds of carbon dioxide emissions each year!

❏ I am turning up my thermostat _____ °F in the summer because of Turn the Tide.

❏ I am turning down my thermostat _____ °F in the winter because of Turn the Tide.

Enter the above numbers into your personal workspace at www.newdream.org or, for those of you keeping score at home, use the following formula and record your results on the chart on page 79.

$$\begin{array}{r} \underline{} \text{° F up in summer} \times 203 \\ + \underline{} \text{° F down in winter} \times 157 \\ \hline \end{array}$$

_____ pounds of carbon dioxide saved each year

❏ I have not taken this action yet.

❏ I don't have air conditioning.

Congratulations! Each extra degree of heat you "put up with" saves 157 pounds of carbon dioxide each summer.

7. Eliminate lawn and garden pesticides.

Cancer rates are rising as pesticides and other toxins pervade our food, water, and bodies. The *Journal of Pesticide Reform* reports that forty percent of all pesticides used in the U.S. mimic hormones in our bodies, causing reproductive disorders and interfering with fetal development. We unintentionally promote pesticide use every time we buy conventionally produced food and clothing (more than 10 percent of the world's pesticides and nearly 25 percent of the world's insecticides are applied to cotton crops).

But Americans also directly apply 70 million pounds of pesticides to home lawns and gardens each year and, in so doing, pollute our precious water resources. If only 1,000 of us stop using pesticides on our gardens and lawns, we'll protect the environment from 950 pounds of toxins each year. If we're also mindful of the pesticide requirements of our other consumer choices, we will boost this figure into the thousands of pounds.

❑ I am eliminating my use of lawn and garden pesticides because of Turn the Tide. My household is saving 15 ounces of pesticides.*

Enter the above number into your personal workspace at www.newdream.org or into the chart on page 79.

❑ I have not taken this action yet.

❑ I didn't use lawn and garden pesticides to begin with.

Congratulations! Pesticide-free households save 15 ounces of toxins, enough to pollute billions of gallons of water.

* This might not sound like much, but consider diazinon, one of the most commonly used home and garden pesticides. One ounce of diazinon is enough to exceed aquatic life guidelines for 94 million gallons of water. This residential chemical has also killed more birds in the last five years than any other pesticide.

8. Install an efficient showerhead and low flow faucet aerators.

Of all natural resources, water is the most essential. But available supply is diminishing rapidly as human populations swell and drain precious aquifers. Consider replacing your washing machine with an efficient front-loading washer, replacing an old toilet with a new ultra low-flow model, fixing leaks around the home (over 25 gallons per day in the average household), and replacing your lawn with a grass species that doesn't require fertilizer or watering. In the short term, pick up faucet aerators for $2-5 apiece and a high-efficiency showerhead for under $20. (These devices give excellent showers and are not to be confused with primitive flow restrictors that simply reduce flow).

INSTALL FAUCET AERATORS

The 1.5 gallons per minute (gpm) model is more than sufficient for bathroom sinks but you may want to go up to the 2.2 gpm model for your kitchen sink.

In less than a year, you'll make that money back through lower utility bills. By reducing demand for hot water, this action also reduces fossil fuel consumption and greenhouse emissions. If only 1,000 of us install faucet aerators and efficient showerheads, we can save nearly 8 million gallons of water and prevent over 450,000 pounds of carbon dioxide emissions each year!

❑ I am installing efficient showerheads and low flow faucet aerators throughout my house because of Turn the Tide. My household is saving 7800 gallons of water and 460 pounds of carbon dioxide each year.

Enter the above number into your personal workspace at www.newdream.org or into the chart on page 79.

❑ I have not taken this action yet.

❑ I already had low flow faucet aerators and high-efficiency showerheads to begin with.

Congratulations! These gadgets save about 7800 gallons of water and 460 pounds of carbon dioxide per year in the average household.

...AND THE LAST SHALL BE FIRST.

This ninth action is worth more than the first eight combined!

9. Convince two friends.

There's an easy way for you to triple the positive impact you are making with these nine actions — convince two friends to join you in your effort! Just pass a copy of this list to receptive friends or tell them to get their own personal workspace at www.newdream.org.

Write the names of people to whom you are giving a copy of these ten workbook pages. Then check them off as they tell you that they are beginning to Turn the Tide.

❏ _____

❏ _____

❏ _____

❏ _____

❏ _____

❏ _____

❏ _____

❏ _____

❏ _____

❏ _____

❏ I have convinced _____ friends to Turn the Tide

_____ friends x 48,500 = _____ gallons of water saved

_____ friends x 3900 = _____ pounds of carbon
dioxide saved

_____ friends ÷ 6 = _____ trees saved

_____ friends x 70 = _____ pounds of grain saved

_____ friends x 12 = _____ pounds of sea life saved

_____ friends x 15 = _____ ounces of toxins avoided

❏ I am the first person in my household to report
taking Turn the Tide actions.

❏ At least one other person in my household has
already reported taking Turn the Tide actions.

Action taken	CO2 saved	Water saved	Trees saved	Grain saved	Sea life saved	Toxins avoided
1. Skip a car trip each week.		▓	▓	▓	▓	▓
2. Eat one less beef meal each week.			▓		▓	▓
3. Don't eat shrimp.	▓	▓	▓	▓		▓
4. Declare your independence from junk mail.				▓	▓	▓
5. Replace four standard light bulbs with CFLs.		▓	▓	▓	▓	▓
6. Move the thermostat 3° F.		▓	▓	▓	▓	▓
7. Eliminate lawn and garden pesticides.	▓	▓	▓	▓	▓	
8. Install an efficient showerhead and low flow faucet aerators.			▓	▓	▓	▓
9. Convince two friends.						
TOTAL SAVINGS						

If you don't have web access to set up your personal workspace, please send a copy of pages 78 and 79 to us so we can calculate the collective impact of everyone Turning the Tide and keep you posted through updates in *Enough!*

MORE FUN, LESS STUFF ACTIVITIES

In our fast-paced culture, it's easy to lose touch with simple pleasures. We work, spend, rush and then collapse each evening, often in front of the television. We scramble to juggle the demands of families, work and over-programmed lives. A family therapist recently was quoted as saying our culture has an attention deficit disorder. Speed, work and the constant race to fit more into each day lock out activities that can bring deeper meaning to our daily lives. Take a minute to ask yourself, "Am I having fun and enjoying my life?"

What makes you laugh? What makes you feel light-hearted? Whatever your passion or pleasure, try to do more of it! For some people, fun is spending time with people they care about. For some, it's close contact with nature. Others find bliss in being with animals or enjoy the thrill of adventure or sport. Some find joy in serving, and many are fulfilled through art, music, or creative pursuits. Here are some examples of "More Fun, Less Stuff" activities you can take advantage of to continue your journey towards a more fulfilling life. We encourage you to share your own suggestions about non-commercial pleasures. Drop us a card or send us an e-mail and we'll share your ideas with others.

Start a Song Circle

Singing is a vibrant part of our history. We sing to celebrate and remember, to proclaim our faith, to entertain, to join families and communities, and to connect with others in recognition of common ground and solidarity. We sing for fun! A song circle is "just a bunch of folks who enjoy getting together to sing," according to the Seattle Folklore Society. Starting a song circle is simple:

✪ Announce a date, time, and location in the classified section of a newspaper or local folk music society newsletter.

✪ Decide whether to invite all instruments, limit instruments to acoustic only, or sing *a cappella* (voice only).

✪ Provide song sheets or booklets.

For more information about creating a local song circle or finding established ones, contact your nearest folk music society.

ADDITIONAL RESOURCE: *Rise Up Singing: The Group Singing Songbook* by Peter Blood and Annie Patterson – Sing Out! Publications.

Spin a Yarn — Storytelling

Storytelling is one of the simplest ways to have free, non-commercial fun and maybe even learn a little something in the process. Why not invite a few friends over, turn out the lights, bring out the candles, and share some homemade stories? Be funny, scary, inspiring, unexpectedly bizarre.

There are over 300 storytelling organizations in the United States. For more information about the rich world of stories, contact:

National Storytelling Association
(800) 525-4514
www.storynet.org

Kick Up Your Heels — Dance

In cities all over the country, it's easy to find places that can teach you to dance. Whether it's moving to African rhythms, twirling around the floor in a Viennese waltz, or stomping to an Irish beat, there are classes that will meet your every need. Many programs are geared specifically to beginners, and the hilarity involved in the learning process is half the fun. Dancing can be more than learning moves to music. It's a great way to increase your heart rate and get exposure to new cultural traditions. It is also an experience that can be shared with friends and family members.

Your local yellow pages may list dancing organizations, but also check the bulletin boards in coffee houses, bookshops, and music stores. Folk societies often have contacts for specific ethnic dances, and clubs may advertise nights specifically for swing or salsa.

ADDITIONAL RESOURCE: Dance America can link you to dancing groups in your area. Write to them at: 512 N. Florida Street, Covington, LA 70433, (800) 224-5534, www.danceamerica.com.

Creative Carving

Durable, beautiful items can be crafted right at home through the art of woodworking — using time-honored traditions such as turning, whittling and carving. From the warm, rich hues of cherry to the clear grains of maple, wood offers a beauty and function for everyone's taste and purpose. Wood can be salvaged from a variety of sites, and more and more places are selling sustainably harvested, certified wood, which prevents clearcutting and other destructive forestry practices. Look for logos from the Forest Stewardship Council, Scientific Certification Systems, or SmartWood for eco-friendly options, and let the fun begin.

Embracing woodworking doesn't mean you have to invest in loads of power tools or fashion a bedroom suite. If you're new to the art, start out small. How about whittling a custom key chain? When your friends and relatives are sick of receiving key chains for their birthdays, move on to wooden spoons! If you don't own tools of your own for the project, you probably have a friend or neighbor who does.

ADDITIONAL RESOURCE: *Basic Bowl Turning* by Judy Ditmer, offers plenty of tips for novice woodworkers. If you're online, check out the Woodworking Catalog, at www.woodworking.com.

Create a Backyard Wildlife Sanctuary

As cities sprawl to accommodate larger populations and more businesses, developments encroach on the habitats of native animals. By planting a few bird- and butterfly-attracting flowers and building some homemade animal feeders, you can create a safe, welcoming environment for displaced animals. Be sure to plant species that are indigenous to your area — once established, native plants don't require fertilizers or pesticides, so they're low-maintenance and safe for the environment.

You can also build feeders and shelters to attract animals. A small, circular hole in a dried-out gourd makes a great hiding spot for finches, swallows and wrens. Scrap wood can easily be turned into funky, creative bird feeders or bat houses. Don't forget to establish your sanctuary in a prominent location, such as outside a kitchen or living room window for optimal viewing delight. Library books on indigenous critters can help you and your family learn to distinguish a nuthatch from a downy, a weasel from a mole. So get outdoors and let the fun begin.

ADDITIONAL RESOURCE: National Wildlife Federation's Backyard Habitat program offers a free brochure, *Creating Habitat for Wildlife at Home, School, Work and in Community*

Write to: NWF, Backyard Habitat Program
8925 Leesburg Pike
Vienna, VA 22184-0001

Or check out their web site at www.nwf.org/habitats/.

"More Fun, Less Stuff" Activities for All Ages

Our members and website visitors have suggested lots of additional ideas, including:

- Paint a picture, mural, or room.

- Visit the library — borrow a book.

- Learn about native trees or flowers in your area — plant something.

- Plan a picnic or barbecue.

- Go bird watching. Learn the names of local birds.

- Write a letter to a friend or relative.

- Bake cookies and bread. Share with a neighbor.

- Join a choir.

- Play cards. Teach a child your favorite games.

What People Are Saying about the Center for a New American Dream

"I teach environmental science at the high school level and have utilized your excellent materials. I appreciate your great work!"

Jack Greene, Logan, Utah

"Through various books, magazines, audio tapes, and video-tapes, I am familiar with your work and the work of your founders, and I am fascinated by everything you stand for. Congratulations to all of you on your excellent, important efforts! Please make me part of your Center's 'family.' "

Robert Gallucci, Waterbury, Connecticut

"I am wild about your work, in all its aspects. It's encouraging to realize that there are far more of us who are able to articulate so clearly and powerfully the real themes and concerns of our time. Thank you for what you do. I'm the Media Specialist for a K-12 charter school and I'm recommending that we develop our curriculum around your materials. Yours is absolutely one of the best web sites going!"

Bliss Bruen, Durango, Colorado

"Ever since I became a reader and a supporter I have wondered how to spread the message and work that you all do. In keeping with the ideals and mission of the Center, I have decided to send each issue, once read, not to the recycling heap, but to friends and family. I ask them in turn to recycle or pass it along after they are through. Keep up the good work."

Simon Tschinkel, New York, New York

"Thank you! It's wonderful to know there are people out there who share the kind of activism I strive for. I'm a student at a 1,000-person public school, and I'm trying to change it from using Styrofoam to trays, to employing composting, and now I want to do something for Buy Nothing Day. Thank you for all of your help. Your wealth of information is more valuable than you could ever imagine. I'm behind you all the way."

Rachel, city and state withheld

"I joined a little over a month ago, prior to giving a lay sermon on holidays and consumerism at my Unitarian Universalist church. I purchased some bumper stickers and holiday booklets to make available to members, and you sent a great package of additional materials! Just wanted to let you know that virtually everything was given away! So thanks, and I look forward to great continued association."

Susan Rogers, Van Nuys, California

"I was so glad to hear about the Center for a New American Dream. I have often said that there was an urgent need for a new American dream, because the current dream of the U.S. has become a nightmare for the world.

Your Center should become one of the main centers in the U.S. I hope that the whole U.S. government and Congress will devote time to formulate the new American dream for the world in the 21st century and the new millennium. May God hear us."

Robert Muller, Chancellor of the UN University for Peace,
Former UN Assistant Secretary General

NEXT STEPS

We hope that the *"More Fun, Less Stuff" Starter Kit* has given you a framework for deciding what changes you want to begin making in a journey towards a more fulfilling and sustainable way of life. There are several additional resources that are available from the Center for a New American Dream:

Step by Step is a brief monthly email service designed to replenish busy individuals through inspiration, action and humor. We provide you with practical tips and ideas for living in ways that enrich your life and make it easy to take action. You can sign up for this free service at www.newdream.org.

"Simplify the Holidays" brochure $2. A 16-page resource full of practical tips for having a more joyful and less consumer-based holiday season.

"Tips for Parenting in a Commercial Culture" brochure $2. Packed with tips and resources to help parents deal with the effects of advertising and marketing on children.

These and other publications can be purchased on our website, www.newdream.org, or by calling us toll-free at (877) 68-DREAM.

Help us Build the Dream

The Center has quadrupled in size in two years. Tens of thousands of people contact us each month. 10,000 agreed to join our action network in its first nine months of existence. There's just a little magic at play here but it only happens through people.

We ask you to help us work for a safe and healthy future. Our aim is to galvanize and support individuals while also working with major organizations, agencies and companies in the quest for a more sustainable culture and economy. It's a big dream but one worth spending time on.

Once you have started on this journey, we promise you won't want to go back. Our members can attest to the fact that the choices they have made to consume differently have directly improved the quality of their lives and the lives of those around them. They have seen a difference, and so will you.

And remember: once you have made a decision to take this whole thing seriously, the Center for a New American Dream is here for you. We have the resources to connect you with others who feel as you do, to offer study materials, parenting tips, and access to companies that provide sustainable products and services. Of course, as we mentioned earlier, this Starter Kit is just that, A STARTER KIT. It doesn't have all the answers, but we hope it helps you to evaluate the priorities in your life, gives you a framework for taking important first steps, and suggests how you can have more fun with less stuff.

What can you do to help us?

✪ Recruit one or more new members for us by using the form on the next page.

✪ Send us the names of people who might like a sample copy of our newsletter, *Enough!* (We will never sell, trade or rent these names to anyone.)

✪ Give a gift membership as a birthday or holiday gift.

✪ Send a financial contribution to support our work.

✪ Send your ideas on how to improve our services and programs.

✪ Most important, consume wisely. If you join with others nationwide in taking these high priority actions, together we will help stem global warming, save trees, and save open space.

KIT EVALUATION

As an organization, the Center for a New American Dream is just getting started. We're still gauging our progress, and we're always trying to improve and refine our programs. Please take a few minutes and give us feedback on this *More Fun, Less Stuff Starter Kit*.

Be Part of the New Dream!

❏ YES! I want to help build the new American dream!

$ _____ **Membership** $30
($15 senior/student/low-income, $50 outside U.S.,
Canada, and Mexico).
Includes quarterly newsletter *Enough!*, our popular *More Fun, Less Stuff Starter Kit*, a More Fun, Less Stuff bumper sticker, and a 50% discount on many Center publications.
❏ Check here if you want to receive our newsletter electronically.
(Please don't forget to give us your email address on page 96)

$ _____ **Donation** $25 $50 $75 $100 $500 $1000
Donate $100 or more (only $8.50/month!) and enjoy
special benefits.

$ _____ **Monthly Donation** $5 $10 $20
Donate monthly and become a member of the New Dream Team!
Donations (minimum $3/month) accepted via electronic transfer
from your checking account (please include a voided check) or via
credit card.

$ _____ **Gift Membership** $25 ($20 each for three or more).
A handwritten card will be sent to the recipient acknowledging your
gift. Please enclose additional sheet for extra names.

Name _____

Address _____

City_____

State_____ Zip _____

$ _____ **TOTAL**

Form continues on reverse

cut along line

Method of Payment:

❏ Check ❏ Credit Card
❏ Electronic Transfer (include voided check)

Card Number _____

Expiration Date _____

Name (as it appears on credit card if applicable)

_____

Signature (required for electronic funds transfer)

_____

Address _____

City _____

State/Province _____

Zip _____ Country _____

Phone/Fax _____

E-mail _____

❏ Check here if you do not want to receive our free
monthly action bulletin Step by Step via email

How did you hear about us?

_____

_____

Please make checks payable to the Center for a New American
Dream and mail to:

The Center for a New American Dream

6930 Carroll Avenue, Suite 900
Takoma Park, MD 20912
PHONE: (301)891-3683 FAX: (301)891-3684
www.newdream.org
newdream@newdream.org